BLACK HAWK

By Maggi Cunningham

DILLON PRESS, INC.
MINNEAPOLIS, MINNESOTA

©1979 by Dillon Press, Inc. All rights reserved
Second printing 1980

Dillon Press, Inc., 500 South Third Street
Minneapolis, Minnesota 55415

Printed in the United States of America

Library of Congress Cataloging in Publication Data

Cunningham, Margaret, 1916
  Black Hawk.

  (The Story of an American Indian)
  SUMMARY: A biography of the last great war leader of
the Sauk whose unsuccessful attempts to keep their home-
lands ended Indian land holdings in the Illinois region.
  1. Black Hawk, Sauk chief, 1767-1838—Juvenile literature.
2. Sauk Indians—Biography—Juvenile literature. [1. Black
Hawk, Sauk chief, 1767-1838. 2. Sauk Indians—Biography.
3. Indians of North America—Biography] I. Title.
E83.83.C86   970'.004'97 [B] [92]   78-26255
ISBN 0-87518-172-4

BLACK HAWK

As the last great war leader of the Sauk, Black Hawk fought against great odds to save the homeland of his people from the land-hungry white settlers. The Sauk, who called themselves the yellow earth people, lived in towns along the valley of the Rock River in what is now Illinois.

At twenty-five, Black Hawk was a famed Sauk warrior and leader who led a devastating campaign against tribes that were invading Sauk hunting grounds. But he did not know how to deal with the Americans, who seized Sauk lands in devious and, to Black Hawk, dishonorable ways. In 1804 William Henry Harrison cajoled and bribed a Sauk delegation into signing a treaty that forfeited the right of the yellow earth people to their homeland.

Black Hawk vowed never to abandon the Sauk homeland and stayed there even when his home town, Saukenuk, was occupied by white squatters. Finally the Illinois militia forced Black Hawk's band to leave Saukenuk and settle to the west on the Iowa River. Before long, however, he led his people back across the Mississippi in an attempt to drive the whites out of Sauk lands. The Americans countered with an army of federal troops and state militia that pursued the desperate Sauk until the Indians were trapped and massacred while trying to recross the Mississippi.

The Sauk had suffered a defeat from which they would never recover. Black Hawk died in 1838 in the Iowa Territory, a lonely and embittered man.

Contents

CHAPTER I

Yellow Earth, Red Earth

On the top of a bluff overlooking the Rock River in Illinois stands a monument to the Sauk warrior and patriot, Black Hawk. The great Indian, carved in stone, looks toward Rock Island in the river and broods over the valley. The Sauk and Fox people believe that long ago, before time was measured in minutes, hours, and days, the Great Spirit chose that fertile valley and the land around it to be their home.

The Great Spirit commanded that the Sauk and Fox, who began life at the same time, must think of themselves as brothers. However, each would have their own sacred things. The Sauk would be known as the yellow earth people and the Fox as the people of the red earth. That was the beginning of peace and friendship between the two tribes.

The Sauk and Fox belonged to the Algonquin language family. "Algonquin" comes from the Indian word, *Alligewinenk,* which means "come together from distant places." The people in this large language family lived in many parts of what is now the eastern United States and Canada.

The Algonquins were divided into nations which were made up of tribes. In the tribes there were many clans, each with its own symbol—an animal, bird, fish, thunder, lightning, or some other powerful thing in the world around them. Each tribe was governed by a council of the sacred clan chiefs, the war chiefs, the heads of families, and the warriors.

For a long time the Sauk and Fox wandered from place to place in search of a home. Every time they tried to settle down, they were driven away by other tribes. Finally, they came to the place that the Great Spirit had chosen for them.

It was a pleasant valley with a river the French would call Riviére de la Roche or River of the Rock. At the place where the river flows into the great Mississippi, an island rose from the waters. There, in the rich valley land near the river, the Sauk and Fox stayed to build their homes and plant their fields.

In the forests and plains along the Rock River and the Mississippi, there were deer, buffalo, bears, and smaller animals that provided food and skins which could be traded or made into clothing. Beavers, otters, and muskrats lived in the many streams that flowed into the rivers. The rivers and streams were filled with many kinds of fish.

North of the valley, the earth held a great store of the mineral, lead. Since it lay close to the surface, the people could dig it out easily. At first they used it to make ornaments for themselves. Later, white traders taught them how to make lead musket balls to use in their guns. Traders who came to Sauk land were happy to take lumps of lead in exchange for goods.

In the valley the soil was rich and fertile. Using the shoulder bones of buffalo and deer, the women broke it up and turned it over. Year after year, they tilled the soil until it was soft as powder and the harvests were great. The

*The Sauk and the Fox believed that the Great Spirit had
commanded them to live as brothers.*

people believed that the Great Spirit had given the care of
all food that grew in the ground—corn, beans, squash,
pumpkins—to the women.

Of all the food crops, corn was the most important. It
might be boiled, roasted, or made into soup or dumplings.
After the kernels were stripped from the cobs, they could
be dried and pounded into meal or stored away for future
use. When the kernels were put on a hot rock, they popped

into fluffy morsels that the children enjoyed as a special treat. Corn even provided its own seed for the next planting. As long as the Sauk and Fox had a good harvest of corn, they knew they would not go hungry.

The harvests were shared among all the people. To have said, "This food belongs to me because I grew it," would have made no sense to the Sauk and Fox. Everything they had, even life, was seen as a gift from the Great Spirit that was meant to be shared.

The Sauk women tilled the soil, raised the crops, gathered the harvests, prepared and stored the food, and reared the children. The mother was in charge of the family home and everything in it. If the mother belonged to the Sauk people, all her children were Sauk. The women also had an important part in tribal government. Unless the women approved, a son could not take his father's place as a sacred clan chief.

The men protected the homes, the fields, and the tribe's hunting grounds. They went into the forests and out on the plains to hunt the game that provided food and skins for clothing and trade.

The Sauk built towns for themselves and surrounded them with well-kept fields. They lived in large, sturdily built lodges with rounded roofs that let the rain and snow roll off easily. Roofs and sides of the lodges were covered with mats woven from dried river rushes or shingles cut from the bark of trees. Most lodges were forty to sixty feet long and had several families living in them. Each family had its own cooking fire in the center of the lodge. Sleeping benches covered with skins and blankets ran along the inside walls.

The Sauk lived in their towns from April to October. When the harvests had been gathered and the geese began to fly south, families went into the forests to build the huts where they would live during the winter hunting season.

People who were too old or weak to move with the rest stayed in the towns. A supply of food for the winter was stored in bark-lined caches in the ground, and some strong young boys stayed behind to look after them. Families went

Each member of a Sauk and Fox family had jobs to do to make sure that their people had enough food, clothing, and shelter.

to the same hunting grounds every winter. If there should be a need, the boys knew where to find them.

Religion played an important part in the daily life of the Sauk. They believed that every person, animal, and thing had its own *manito,* or guardian spirit, which came directly from the Great Spirit. When a hunter killed a bear, a deer, a buffalo, or any animal, he thanked the *manito* of the animal for the gifts it was giving to the people.

Children began learning the religion of their people at an early age. Boys were taught to fast and to keep holy vigils to bring their souls closer to the Great Spirit. Then, when a boy grew old enough, he made a special vigil quest. The Great Spirit would show him his personal *manito,* which would stay with him the rest of his life. At that time, he chose his manhood name and began to collect the sacred things that would go into his medicine bag.

Although the Sauk were a peaceful people, sometimes they had to go to war to defend their hunting grounds or their towns. Neighboring tribes such as the Osage raided Sauk lands. The Sauk were noted for their courage, and they believed that every raid should be answered by a counter raid to uphold the honor of their people. When another tribe invaded Sauk lands, a council was called to decide what action to take. Often a war party was sent out to meet the enemy.

Warfare had its own rules of conduct. Killing an enemy was not an end in itself. In war, a Sauk gained honor if he could count coup. That meant that he had touched an armed enemy and lived to tell about it. Counting coup earned a warrior the right to wear an eagle feather in his crest.

These were the people of the Sauk warrior and patriot, Black Hawk. They lived happily and well in the valley of the Rock River. But with the coming of the first white people, they learned to use guns as well as bows and arrows, and to ride horses to hunt and to make war.

Guns were brought to the Sauk by white traders who offered them in exchange for furs and lead. The yellow earth people found out that the new weapons could bring down a bear, a deer, or a buffalo at a greater distance than a bow and arrow. And, in war, the guns would do the same to people.

Tribes of the Siouan language family brought horses to the plains from the Spaniards in the Southwest. Soon the tribes of the Algonquin language family learned that a warrior or a hunter riding a strong horse traveled more quickly than if he went on foot. By 1800 it was hard for the Sauk to remember how life had been without horses. The more horses a man had, the richer he was.

When Black Hawk was born in 1767, the ancient ways of the yellow earth people were beginning to change because of guns and horses. He was to grow up to face the greatest danger of all—the white people who called themselves Americans.

CHAPTER II

The Young
Warrior

Black Hawk grew up in Saukenuk, the largest town of the Sauk people, located two miles above the place where the Rock River flows into the Mississippi. Three thousand people lived in lodges along straight streets that came together at a large square in the center of the well-planned town. A council lodge for talk about tribal affairs stood at the edge of the square. Each clan in the town had its own lodge where its sacred things were kept and secret rites were performed.

The childhood of Black Hawk was like that of other Sauk boys. When a child was born, the parents brought a food offering to the oldest person in the father's clan so that the baby would receive the blessing of the Great Spirit. All children were treasured, and no father ever punished his own son. That was the duty of an uncle or other relative.

When a boy was about five years old, he was given a sheaf of blunted arrows and a bow that was the right size for him to handle. He was taught how to aim and shoot at targets that didn't move. Later, he would learn how to hit swinging bundles of straw. When he was good enough, he would try his luck at hunting small animals that would help to feed and clothe his family.

The lodges of Saukenuk looked much like these Sauk homes.

It was a proud day for everybody when a boy brought home the first deer he had killed. His mother removed the skin and would tan it for him to keep. When she cooked the meat, his father invited friends and relatives for a feast. A boy never ate the meat of his first deer. Instead, he stood beside his father and listened while the guests admired him and talked about the great things he would do when he was grown up. Listening to the praise was better than eating!

Black Hawk's father, Pyesa, belonged to the Thunder clan. The men of Thunder thought so much of him that they chose him to be the keeper of the clan's sacred medicine bundle. Members of the Thunder clan could not be chiefs. However, no other Sauk clan was better at hunting, making war if they had to, and raiding the horse herds of other nations. The Sauk, Osage, Kickapoo, and Winnebago raided each other's herds so often that it was like constant trading back and forth.

A horse raid was always carried out on foot. The raiders would tie their own mounts at a place that was downwind from the target herd. Horses were taken one at a time. To try to get away with several at once might frighten the animals and alert the enemy.

One horse was quietly separated from the rest of the herd. A rawhide rope was thrown around its neck for a halter, and a loop was hooked over its lower lip to act as a bridle. After that, the prize was ready to be led or ridden away to the place where the raiders' own horses were hidden. To keep the stolen horse from running away, it was tied, neck to neck, to a gentle mare and coaxed along to its new home.

The men of the Thunder clan were pleased with the way that young Black Hawk was growing into a fine hunter and raider. When he was fifteen, they asked him to ride along with a war party against the Osage. Black Hawk fought bravely by the side of Pyesa. Two years later he had become a respected warrior. The young man had counted coup many times and had earned the right to wear eagle feathers in his crest.

One day, word came that a band of one hundred Osage

had crossed the Mississippi and set up an armed camp in the Sauk hunting grounds. The Osage, who belonged to the Siouan language family, were longtime enemies of the yellow earth people. Black Hawk had never led a war party, but the men of Thunder thought he should have a chance. The Fox clan, which gave the nation its war chiefs, agreed.

Black Hawk took a party of young warriors into battle with the Osage invaders and defeated them soundly. Every man in the Sauk band counted coup. The Sauk code of honor called for the enemy to be punished and taught to stay away from Sauk hunting grounds. Black Hawk, pleased with himself after his victory, led another war party to raid an Osage village.

The Sauk rode their horses right up to the first wigwams, ready to storm their way in, when they stopped. There was nobody there. Their overeager young leader had brought them to a deserted village!

The men in the war party were disgusted. After all that time and trouble, they had nothing to show for their efforts. Soon most of them left Black Hawk, but five young warriors stayed with him. The rest were on their way home where they would be quick to tell everybody about the wild goose chase.

Black Hawk motioned for the faithful five to follow him into the village. The ashes from the cooking pots were still wet from the water that had been poured over them to put out the fires. Somehow, the people must have found out that the war party was coming and run away to hide. Carefully and quietly, the young leader and his five followers searched for a clue to the way they had gone.

By the time the Sauk warriors who had left him got home, Black Hawk was right on their heels. He had tracked down the Osage, and now he was leading a dozen captured horses loaded with bundles of goods. It would be a long time before a Sauk warrior left him again.

One successful raid followed another. Many fine horses were added to the herds of the yellow earth people. Enemies began to be careful not to offend the Sauk because their war party might be led by a famous young warrior called Black Hawk.

On most raids Pyesa went along with Black Hawk. He was proud of his son's achievements as a young warrior and leader. Then, in a battle against the Cherokees, seven Sauk were killed. One of the seven was Pyesa.

When the war party returned to Saukenuk, Black Hawk went to the keepers of the sacred things of the clans to which the dead warriors belonged. He asked their permission to call for a Medicine Dance of the Brave for each man. He himself led the dancers.

The Medicine Dance of the Brave was the highest honor the Sauk could offer a fallen warrior. It followed a pattern that went back to the beginnings of the yellow earth people.

When a warrior died in battle, his widow hung his medicine bag on a green bush in front of her house. She sat in the doorway and wept. Every day, for fifteen days, the friends of the dead man came to dance and throw presents. The gifts showed respect for the warrior's spirit and gave comfort to his family.

When all the dances were finished, Black Hawk began his own period of mourning for his father. He put away his ornaments and his bright red paint and blackened his face with charcoal. Then, he went away from his people to fast and pray to the Great Spirit.

Among the Sauk, the usual period of mourning lasted for six months to a year. Black Hawk spent five years alone in the forest and on the plains seeking strength and guidance from the Great Spirit. He had much to learn, for now he was the keeper of the sacred medicine bundle of the Thunder clan. During that hard and lonely time, Black Hawk learned about the ancient laws of nature, healing powders and herbs, and signs from Mother Earth and Father Sky.

When he returned, he came as an older and wiser man, ready to act as the keeper of the medicine. He carried a food gift to the oldest person in the Thunder clan, and his friends welcomed him back to Saukenuk.

Black Hawk was eager to prove that none of his warrior's skill and courage had been lost. The Osage had been raiding the towns and hunting grounds of the Sauk while he had been away. Black Hawk led a war party that destroyed an Osage village and captured many fine horses.

Next, he set out to punish the Cherokees who had killed his father. His war party came upon a small band of the enemy. Since there were only five Cherokees, Black Hawk decided to insult them instead of attacking. He and the Sauk warriors sneered at them and rode away as if they thought the Cherokees weren't worthy of notice. The Cherokees recognized Black Hawk, and they were glad to get off with no more than an insult.

At twenty-five, Black Hawk was a famed warrior and leader of his people. For the next ten years, he led the campaign against the nearby tribes that were raiding Sauk and Fox lands. The Sauk won many battles, and finally the raids stopped.

It was a happy time for Black Hawk and his people. Later

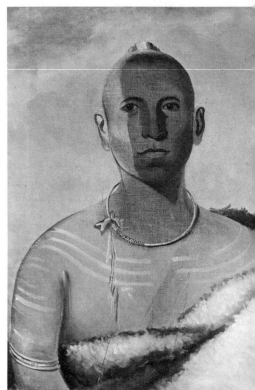

Black Hawk was proud of his two sons, Roaring Thunder and Whirling Thunder.

in his life he would tell about it in his autobiography: "Our enemies having now been driven from our hunting grounds, with so great a loss . . . we returned, in peace, to our villages . . . . We always had plenty—our children never cried with hunger, nor our people were ever in want. Here our village had stood for more than a hundred years, during all which time we were the undisputed possessors of the valley of the Mississippi . . . about seven hundred miles in length."

In Saukenuk Black Hawk settled down to marry Singing Bird. He was proud of their two sons, Whirling Thunder and Roaring Thunder, and the three children who came after them. But the peaceful times at home would not last for long.

CHAPTER III

A Troubled
Time

Life for the Sauk and Fox people had passed in much the same way for many, many years. The changes caused by horses and guns were fitted in with the ancient customs. Some good could be found in both the old and new ways.

In the past many whites had come and gone among the peoples of the yellow earth and the red earth. The Spanish came looking for gold and lost interest when they didn't find any. The French and British traded goods for furs and lead and went away. But the Americans were different. They came to take over the land, settle on it, and stay.

In 1803 the French sold a vast region in the middle of North America to the United States. After the sale the whites talked about something they called the Louisiana Purchase. Since the eastern boundary of the Purchase was not clearly set down, there was nothing to stop the Americans from claiming the land on both sides of the Mississippi River. White people brought their families, wagons, plows, and farm animals. They began to build cabins in the forest, on the plains, and even in the valley of the Rock River.

The Sauk and Fox were angered by the invasion of their hunting grounds. Bad feeling grew between them and the

Americans when a white man was caught beating an Indian child and was killed by the child's father. According to Sauk custom, when a man killed someone by accident or in anger, he made a gift to the dead person's family as a gesture of peace. The Sauk who had defended his child took a gift to the Place of Shallow Water on the Mississippi where the whites had built the town of Saint Louis.

Three friends and a Sauk chief named Jumping Fish went with him. In Saint Louis white officials accepted the gift but threw the Sauk who brought it in jail.

Jumping Fish and the three Sauk began a desperate search for someone who could help their friend. They learned that the governor of the Indiana Territory, William Henry Harrison, was in Saint Louis on a mission for President Thomas Jefferson. He had come to make treaties with the American Indians who were living on land the United States claimed through the Louisiana Purchase.

The Sauk went to see Harrison to request the release of their friend. Harrison listened politely and asked them to come back in a couple of days.

On November 4, 1804, he showed the Sauk a piece of parchment written in a strange language. Since Jumping Fish was a chief, Harrison told him to put his sign on the parchment. He told the Sauk chief that if he signed, their friend would be released from prison.

Jumping Fish couldn't read the words that were written on the parchment. When he put his sign to it, nobody told him it was a treaty that would give all the Sauk and Fox lands east of the Mississippi between the Wisconsin and Illinois rivers to the United States. That included Saukenuk, the home of Black Hawk!

In return for the land, the government promised to pay the Sauk and Fox one thousand dollars every year. Also, the Indians could live on the land "until it was needed for settlement." By the Treaty of 1804, Harrison delivered 15 million acres of Indian land to the land-hungry Americans.

Harrison must have known that, according to Sauk and Fox laws and customs, the treaty was worthless. A real treaty must be talked about in the council lodge. It had to bear the signs of many chiefs—not just one. Besides, the Treaty of 1804 had a clause that the Sauk and Fox would have turned down at once if they had been asked about it. It said that they must keep the peace with their enemies, the Osage!

Black Hawk declared that the Treaty of 1804 was not a true one, and he vowed never to honor it. Most of the chiefs, warriors, and family heads agreed with him.

One man, Keokuk, wouldn't say yes or no. Keokuk belonged to the Fox clan that gave war chiefs to the Sauk, but he was content to be the guest keeper for the clan. It was a position of little importance and did not take much work. That gave Keokuk, who was a sly and crafty man, plenty of time to make clever deals that would show a profit for him. Black Hawk looked on the man as a shirker who did not fulfill his duty to the Sauk people. He and Keokuk were never friends.

The Americans hailed the treaty, and before long white settlers began to come into Sauk and Fox lands. The first to show up were the squatters. Squatters were really land thieves. They didn't buy the land from anybody or use a legal means to stake their claims. They boldly moved onto a piece of land that they liked and drove everybody else

The sly and crafty Keokuk tried to gain power and money for himself at the expense of the Sauk people.

away. They chopped down the trees, killed the game animals, and fought with the Indians who lived nearby.

Squatters were followed by whites who planned to make fortunes by buying and selling land. They bought up whole tracts from the U.S. government and sold them off in small parcels to homesteaders. As the homesteaders moved in, the squatters pushed deeper into Indian lands.

The Sauk and Fox were given no say in this carving up of their fields and hunting grounds. When they tried to buy their own land, the government forbade the sale. Angered and uneasy, they watched for the white settlers' next move.

British traders still came to Saukenuk to trade their goods for lead and furs. It was a good business, and the Americans wanted to take the rich fur trade for themselves.

In 1806 an American army captain, Zebulon Pike, came to Saukenuk with an exploring party to find the source of the

Mississippi. He was surprised and angry when he saw a British flag flying over the town. According to the Treaty of 1804, Saukenuk was in United States territory. Captain Pike demanded that the flag be taken down. He promised that the president would send an American flag to take its place.

The people of Saukenuk brought the matter to Black Hawk. Black Hawk had known many of the British traders for a long time. They were his friends, but he knew that the Sauk would be better off if they were friends with the Americans, too. Black Hawk told Pike that the Sauk would be honored to show the American flag. It could fly right alongside the British banner. Pike was not happy with this plan, but he agreed to it and went on his way.

Two years after Pike left, the American army arrived in force. Soldiers built Fort Madison on the Mississippi a hundred miles south of Saukenuk. When the United States and Great Britain went to war in 1812, the yellow earth people had a difficult choice to make. They were longtime friends of the British, but the Americans were getting stronger and might attack their towns if the Sauk sided with the British forces. Black Hawk said the Sauk would be better off if they didn't favor one side or the other.

Nevertheless, the War of 1812 split the Sauk people into two groups. The sly and crafty Keokuk saw a chance to make himself popular with the American officers stationed at Fort Madison. He made a great show of forming a "peace party." With a small group of followers, he moved out of Saukenuk and placed himself under the protection of the U.S. government. To an outsider, it looked as if Keokuk, not Black Hawk, was in favor of keeping the peace.

The year 1812 brought bad weather. When the harvest was gathered, it was too small to feed the people during the winter. Black Hawk asked a U.S. government agent at Fort Madison if the Sauk could get food and weapons in exchange for trade goods that they would bring in the next spring. The agent said no.

The Sauk would have little to eat that winter unless they could find another source of food. When hope was almost gone, a British trader made his way up the Rock River with a fleet of canoes loaded with supplies. He knew about the trouble the Sauk were having with the Americans, and he urged Black Hawk to side with the British in the war.

Black Hawk felt he had a debt of honor. It was the British—not the Americans—who were giving his people food to live on during the long winter. So, with a war party of two hundred Sauk and Fox, Black Hawk headed north to Green Bay in what is now Wisconsin. There, a trader, Robert Dickson, was gathering an Indian force to fight for the British.

Dickson welcomed the famous Sauk leader and made him the head of the Indian force at Green Bay. Black Hawk and his warriors became known as the British Band. For a time, using arms supplied by the British, they raided frontier settlements in Wisconsin. Then they went to join Tecumseh's Indian force, which along with the British had captured Detroit from the Americans. For years Tecumseh had tried to unite Indian tribes against American attempts to seize their lands. The great Shawnee war chief had come to Saukenuk a few years before, and Black Hawk knew and respected him.

The British Band fought bravely in the battle at the

River Raisin in which the British and Indians defeated an army of Kentuckians. Later Black Hawk joined Tecumseh and the British in the siege of Fort Meigs and Fort Stephenson in Ohio.. The Indian forces fought with skill and courage, but the English leader, General Procter, would not commit his soldiers to a full-scale battle. After a long siege, the British forces went back to Detroit and soon retreated into Canada. Tecumseh was killed in the Battle of the Thames in 1814. Black Hawk's band left the war and returned to Saukenuk.

At home Black Hawk found that things had changed while he had been away. Keokuk had caught the attention of the Americans. They looked on him as a friend and planned to appoint him as the head chief of all the Sauk and Fox. Black Hawk was deeply angered.

At this time the war between the two white nations was still going on. The British asked Black Hawk to help them fight the Americans to the north at Prairie du Chien. With the aid of the British Band, they were able to defeat the U.S. troops. This aid so angered the Americans that they sent an army north to destroy the Sauk towns on the Rock River.

News of the approaching army caused Sauk and Fox and even Winnebago and Dakota warriors to hurry to Saukenuk to help Black Hawk defend the homeland of his people. The British sent a small force with big guns. When the Americans camped on an island near the mouth of the Rock River, the Indians attacked. They crossed the river in canoes in the pre-dawn darkness and fell upon the startled U.S. troops. From the shore the British guns shelled the American boats with deadly fire that threatened to sink

Zachary Taylor led the Americans in an attempt to seize Saukenuk.

them. The American commander, Major Zachary Taylor, ordered a hasty retreat down the Mississippi toward Saint Louis.

By the end of the war, Black Hawk's warriors had made it possible for the British to control the entire upper Mississippi Valley. But what had been won in battle, was lost at the treaty table. By the terms of the treaty that ended the war, the British gave up all claims to the land south of the Great Lakes. A few strokes of a goose quill pen had delivered the Sauk and their lands firmly into the hands of the Americans.

CHAPTER IV

The Challenged Hawk

The peace between the two white nations meant trouble for Black Hawk's people. With the end of the war, the Americans began building a line of forts that stretched from the Great Lakes to the Mississippi River. More and more white settlers came, and towns grew up around the forts.

Fort Armstrong was built right next to Saukenuk on Rock Island. In his autobiography Black Hawk told how his people felt about the soldiers near their home. "We were very sorry, as this was the best island on the Mississippi, and had long been the resort of our young people during the summer. It was our garden (like the white people have near to their big villages) which supplied us with strawberries, blackberries, gooseberries, plums, apples, and nuts of different kinds; and its waters supplied us with fine fish, being situated in the rapids of the river. In my early life, I spent many happy days on this island."

The U.S. government declared that the area between the Mississippi and Illinois rivers was a "military tract" where grants of land would be given to men who had fought in the war. Hunting grounds of the Sauk and Fox were in this tract. Soon the deer, bear, and buffalo began to disappear

American soldiers built Fort Armstrong on the island where Black Hawk spent many happy days during his childhood.

from the land east of the Mississippi. Black Hawk's people began to go west of the river for their winter hunt, but this put them on the hunting grounds of the Dakota. They had little choice—either they could fight the Dakota or go hungry.

American veterans from the war claimed land they never expected to see, much less live on. When they didn't pay the taxes, the land was put up for public sale. Land grabbers bought it up and sold it to homesteaders. Once again, squatters moved ahead of the homesteaders and destroyed the things the Sauk and Fox needed to live.

In the spring of 1822, the Americans found out about the deposits of lead ore on Sauk land. When the settlers heard that the Sauk were mining many tons of lead each year, the government began leasing out tracts of land.

A lead boom was on. Mining camps grew up at Galena and Fort Clark, and the white miners wanted the Indians out of the way. For the first time, someone proposed that the Sauk should be moved and resettled on the west bank of the Mississippi.

Black Hawk planned to fight any attempt the whites might make to force the Sauk to leave their homes. He had to deal, however, with the growing power of Keokuk.

Keokuk had become a crafty trader as well as a good politician. His selling of whiskey to the Sauk had made the people need him in a new and terrible way. Many of them had become addicted to alcohol. Under its influence they did things that made them ashamed when they sobered up. To forget what they had done, they got drunk again. Before long, whiskey became so important to some of the people that they were easy to cheat. The finest pelts, guns, traps, anything of value, would be traded for a jug of cheap whiskey. Drinking caused many Sauk to go into debt to the storekeepers at the trading posts.

Black Hawk broke every cask of the "bad medicine" he could find while Keokuk used it to make money for himself.

Storekeepers bought the whiskey for twenty-five cents a gallon and sold it to the Sauk for twenty dollars. Keokuk made a deal with the Americans to share in the profits.

Along with the sale of whiskey, Keokuk had another way to make money. Fine horses from the ranches in the Southwest were brought into the valley of the Rock River. The Americans turned that market over to their favorite, Keokuk. Between the profits from horses and whiskey, that unimportant guest-keeper was becoming the richest man in the Sauk tribe.

People began to think of Keokuk as a man of good luck. Some gathered around him, hoping to share his fortune. Others clung to the sacred customs of the yellow earth people. They did not drink whiskey or go into debt to the storekeepers, and Black Hawk was their leader.

The Americans had a reason for favoring Keokuk. If he became the most powerful leader of the Sauk, it would be easier to get the Sauk to leave their homeland. But if the Americans had to deal with Black Hawk, they knew it would be hard to force the Sauk off their land.

The first test of leadership came when the American agent at the fort on Rock Island met with the Sauk and told them they would have to leave by the spring of 1829. By this time, in Black Hawk's words, "We were a divided people, forming two parties. Keokuk being at the head of one, willing to barter our rights merely for the good opinion of the whites; and cowardly enough to desert our village to them. I was at the head of the other party, and was determined to hold on to my village although I had been ordered to leave it. . . . It was here that I was born, and here lie the bones of many friends and relations."

Many of the Sauk looked to Keokuk as their leader because the Americans favored him and he had power and money.

After this, Keokuk's band left Saukenuk and settled to the west of the Mississippi River. Black Hawk vowed never to leave the Sauk homeland. The next spring, after the winter hunting season, he led his loyal followers back to Saukenuk as usual.

When the Sauk returned, they hardly recognized their town. Rubbish filled the streets, fences surrounded their fields, and smoke was coming out of the smoke-holes of houses that should have been empty. When the Sauk tried to enter their homes, they were met at the doors by white men with guns. Squatters had taken over the town of Saukenuk!

The old people had been crowded into one wickiup. Their food had been stolen, and the squatters had threatened to kill them if any of the young men ran away to tell Black Hawk about what was happening.

When the Sauk tried to get the bundles of furs they had left stored in their houses, they were threatened. The women asked for the jars of seed that they needed for the spring planting. The squatters drove them off.

The white people claimed that, as American citizens, they could take over the land on which the town had been built. Since the Sauk were not citizens of the United States, they had no rights.

Black Hawk made up his mind that if needed, he would use force to clear the squatters out of Saukenuk. The young warriors and his old friends from the British Band agreed with him. Before long the squatters began to lose their courage. They sent a message to John Reynolds, the governor of Illinois, asking for help.

Governor Reynolds was a country lawyer and a shrewd

politician who prided himself on giving the voters whatever they wanted. When he had been a young man, Reynolds had joined a band of whites who ranged over the country-side, frightening the Indians. From that adventure, he earned his nickname, The Old Ranger.

Reynolds sent word back to Saukenuk that he was sending the militia to protect the citizens of the State of Illinois. He promised that the Sauk would be moved out and resettled on the west side of the Mississippi River, "dead or alive!"

Often the militia was made up of men who were untrained and hard to control. They enlisted for a term of thirty days. Each man brought his own gun and, if he had one, his own horse. Since most were poor, they were content to receive a few pennies a day and a jug of whiskey.

Reynolds had called up the militia without telling the U.S. military commander of the area, General Edmund P. Gaines. When the general heard about the planned march on Saukenuk, he was worried. He had a professional soldier's contempt for the governor's ragtag band, and he knew, from experience, that there would be a few scalp hunters among the men who enlisted. Some traders in the area would pay only five dollars for a prime wolf pelt, but they'd give forty dollars for an Indian scalp.

The general rode hard to reach Saukenuk before the militia. He was received as an honored guest, and a council was called to hear what he had to say. Keokuk and some of his followers came back to Saukenuk for the council. Gaines sat with the sacred chiefs, the war chiefs, the warriors, and the heads of families, but he knew that Black Hawk was the man he must convince.

Gaines told Black Hawk that the lives of his people were in danger. He said that it would be better for all the Sauk to cross the Mississippi and live together on the Iowa River. There, he said, they could build new homes, plant their fields, and nobody would trouble them. Gaines must have forgotten that the land to the west was used by the Iowa, Osage, Dakota, and other tribes. Already the Sauk who lived there had problems. The soil was difficult to break up and the crops were poor.

Black Hawk stood up to reply to the general. "We have never sold our country," he said. "We are determined to hold on to our village." Angered, Gaines shouted, "Who is Black Hawk? Who is Black Hawk?" Black Hawk said proudly, "I am a Sauk! My forefathers were Sauk! And all the nations call me a Sauk!" The general spoke again. "I came here, neither to beg nor hire you to leave your village. My business is to remove you, peaceably if I can, but forcibly if I must. I will now give you two days to remove, and if you do not cross the Mississippi within that time, I will adopt measures to force you away!"

About one-third of the Sauk at the council, led by Keokuk and his followers, agreed that all the Sauk should make the move to the Iowa River. The rest sided with Black Hawk.

Unable to convince Black Hawk to leave Saukenuk, General Gaines allowed the Illinois militia to march on the town. They attacked at dawn on June 25, 1831. But when the Americans swept into the village, they found it empty. Black Hawk's scouts had warned him of the attack, and during the night he had led his people across the Mississippi to safety. Furious, the militia destroyed everything in sight and burned Saukenuk to the ground.

General Gaines sent an urgent message to Black Hawk, insisting on another council. On June 30 Black Hawk and his followers met the general at Fort Armstrong. They were all wearing full war dress, but they were carrying a flag of truce. Voices grew loud. The arguments were fierce. In the end, Black Hawk and the chiefs who had come with him put their signs on the treaty that Gaines offered them.

The Sauk agreed to stop all fighting and move to the west side of the Mississippi. Black Hawk was the last to put his sign on the treaty. He did it with such angry force that he broke the goose quill pen. "Why did the Great Spirit ever send the white man to this island," he would ask years later, "to introduce us to poisonous liquors, disease, and death?"

The next winter was a terrible time. The Sauk had crossed the river too late to plant crops even if the ground could have been prepared. They hardly had time to build simple shelters for themselves before the hard winter of the plains was upon them.

Starving and with very little of value, the Sauk went into the trading posts to ask for enough corn to see them through the cold weather. The storekeepers reminded them of the overdue debts of some of the tribe and offered them whiskey. They were insulted and sent away hungry.

Other tribes and nations tried to sneak food to Black Hawk and his people, but Keokuk, with the help of the Americans, set himself up as the one to receive the gifts. He gave them only to those who would join his party. Many of the Sauk did not live through that winter.

CHAPTER V

Return of the Yellow Earth People

After the Sauk were driven from their homes, Black Hawk tried the American way of sending a message written with a goose quill pen. He had a friend write a letter which was sent to the U.S. government at Saint Louis. In the letter Black Hawk described how white settlers had come into Saukenuk and how the soldiers had burned the homes of his people. He told about the sale of whiskey, which made it easy for whites to steal from the Sauk. He mourned the destruction of the Sauk burial grounds. Now women had no place to go to weep for their lost children. Men had nowhere to grieve for their fathers.

The government replied that the Treaty of 1804 gave Sauk land to the United States. The yellow earth people had no claim to it.

It was a hard time for Black Hawk. His people were split between Keokuk's "peace" party and his own followers, who feared and hated the Americans. A divided people would have a hard time taking back its homeland. Black Hawk knew that many tribes were suffering from the actions of the Americans. If the Indians could stop fighting each other and unite, he believed that they could drive out the white settlers.

During the winter Black Hawk sent secret messengers to neighboring tribes. They carried his plan for a single fighting force to make the whites leave the Indian lands. Everywhere they went, the messengers were treated with great politeness. The tribes they visited encouraged Black Hawk to go ahead with his plan.

In the spring the Winnebago, who lived north of the Sauk in what is now Wisconsin, invited Black Hawk and his people to use their land to plant crops. Soon Governor Reynolds heard about the offer. He sent word to Black Hawk to stay where he was until the governor gave him permission to move or he had a pass signed by the president.

On April 5, 1832, the Sauk leader defied the order of Governor Reynolds and led his people across the Mississippi River to the Illinois side. Five hundred seasoned warriors, their wives, children, and aged parents, about two thousand people in all, followed Black Hawk. He was sure that armed Winnebago and Potowatomi would be on the other side to meet him. When the Sauk arrived, no one was there.

During the next few days, small bands of warriors came to join the Sauk, but not in the numbers Black Hawk had hoped for. It turned out that the tribes were afraid. Already they had felt the heavy hand of the American government when they had tried to stand up for their rights. They wished Black Hawk well with his plan, but they felt safer if they took no part in it.

Now that Black Hawk was back on Sauk land, he meant to stay there. He led his people north and east along the Rock River, looking for a place where they could settle for the summer. Once crops were planted, the Sauk would feel that they had come back home.

Several Sauk chiefs brought bands of warriors to join Black Hawk. Although these men were chiefs and Black Hawk did not belong to a chieftain clan, they looked to him as their leader. His age and experience commanded respect. Black Hawk, however, didn't look to those men for advice. Instead, he listened to Neapope and White Cloud, who was called the Prophet.

Neapope was a dreamer, a troublemaker, and a teller of tales. He placed himself at Black Hawk's side and spoke out boldly in councils. Since Neapope belonged to a clan that produced sacred chiefs, Black Hawk believed that the *manito* of the young man was strong.

The Prophet, a medicine man, was part Sauk and part Winnebago. He went against custom by letting his hair grow to cover his whole head. The Prophet claimed the wand he carried had healing powers and that he controlled certain spirits that would do whatever he asked. He attached himself to Black Hawk by appealing to the leader's deep religious beliefs.

The Prophet promised Black Hawk that the Great Spirit was going to send a terrible sickness to the white people which would destroy them. Neapope told him that the British were coming to help defeat the Americans. Like many troubled leaders, Black Hawk believed the two men because they told him what he wanted to hear.

Black Hawk was still looking for a place for his people to settle and plant crops when Governor Reynolds found out that the Sauk leader had dared to cross the Mississippi. He demanded help from the federal government in dealing with the rebellious Sauk and called out the Illinois militia. This time the militiamen elected Sam Whiteside, an old

Even though the Americans had told Black Hawk to stay west of the Mississippi, he led his people back to the valley of the Rock River.

friend of the governor from his days as a ranger, to be their general. There was nothing Sam Whiteside enjoyed more than fighting Indians.

The federal government sent troops up the Mississippi from Saint Louis. Both the regular army and the Illinois militia were put under the command of Brevet General Henry Atkinson at Fort Armstrong.

Atkinson was a general only by courtesy. His brevet commission gave him the right to use the title, but his military rank and pay were those of a colonel. He had spent most of his career behind a desk and had little experience in the field. However, he had powerful friends who put his name up for command of the campaign against Black Hawk.

The militiamen and the regular army troops disliked each other. Before they could hope to capture Black Hawk, General Atkinson faced the task of getting them to work together. It didn't help when Governor Reynolds rode in to join his old friend, Sam Whiteside.

Word reached Fort Armstrong that the Sauk had made camp near the Rock River on a stream called Sycamore Creek, a two-day march away. Whiteside drew rations for the militia and galloped off, leaving the regular army troops to follow in their boats.

Black Hawk's camp was a sad place. Rain had been falling for days, and food was scarce. The people had been on the move constantly since crossing the Mississippi. They had had no chance to put in crops. They were hungry.

Black Hawk was discouraged. The British help which Neapope had promised had not come. The spirits of the Prophet had not destroyed the white people. Black Hawk's scouts told him that white soldiers were on his trail.

The time had come when the Sauk leader would have welcomed a truce. If the Americans offered peace and food for his people, he would have led them back to the Iowa River.

Most of Black Hawk's warriors were off looking for any game animals or edible roots they could find when a scout rode into camp. He brought word that three or four hundred Americans had settled for the night at a place only a few miles away. Black Hawk believed that they would come, ready for battle, the next morning. His people were too hungry to fight. He decided to send three young men with a flag of truce to invite the Americans to a council. After they left he sent five warriors to watch the flag bearers.

It was a wet, cold, dark night. Sentries posted around the militiamen's camp watched their companions warming themselves at the fires while they stood out in the rain. One by one, they left their posts and joined the nearest groups where whiskey jugs were passed from mouth to mouth to ward off the chill.

When three Indians walked into the camp, the soldiers panicked. Not even the commanding officer, Major Isaiah Stillman, took the time to think about the meaning of the flag of truce they held over their heads.

A drunken militiaman picked up his gun and fired a shot that hit and killed the flag-bearer. More shots brought down the other two Indians. The Sauk warriors who had trailed along to watch rode back to Black Hawk's camp with the news of what had happened.

Black Hawk had been getting ready to receive the Americans for a council. When he heard about what had happened to his peace mission, he was shocked and angry. Although there were only about forty warriors around at the time, he gave the command to ride to the enemy's camp.

The warriors said goodbye to their families. They were sure they were riding to their deaths, but Sauk honor was at stake. They were proud to be in the war party.

Meanwhile, the militiamen were milling around, trying to figure out what was happening. They thought they were surrounded by hostile Indians and began shooting at anything that moved. Many men were hit by their friends. When they saw Black Hawk coming toward them with his handful of warriors, they were sure the end had come.

The militiamen fled, leaving everything behind. Stillman's men went past him at a dead run. They neither heard nor cared about his shouted commands. After a look around, Stillman himself galloped off to join them.

Black Hawk and his warriors watched the retreat in amazement. The Americans were camped in a place that would have been easy to defend. When the soldiers gave up so quickly, the Sauk didn't know what to make of it.

The body of the young Sauk who had carried the white flag was lifted from the ground. Carrying the wounded men on horses, the party returned to camp. They took along the clothing, guns, ammunition, and food the Americans had left behind. The people in Black Hawk's camp could use all of it.

After that night, Sycamore Creek had a new name. It was called Stillman's Run.

CHAPTER VI

The Black Hawk War

News of what had happened at Stillman's Run spread quickly. Soon groups of Winnebago and Potowatomi warriors found the courage to join Black Hawk. As the militiamen went back to their homes, they told their own stories about Stillman's Run. Black Hawk's forty warriors grew into a band of Indians so big that it couldn't be counted. They made up tales about what happened and told them as facts. Nobody said anything about the flag of truce that the three young Sauk had carried into the American camp.

The white settlers believed the stories the militiamen told, and they were afraid. Maybe the Indians were getting ready to attack! Villages were turned into forts. People looked for hostile Indians behind every tree and walked around with guns under their arms. Politicians and newspaper writers demanded that General Atkinson put an end to the Indian danger and do it at once.

The general moved out of Fort Armstrong and had his soldiers build an earthen fort a short distance up the Rock River. Governor Reynolds went with him. The governor was worried about his militia. Many who had been at Stillman's Run had lost their taste for fighting Indians. At the end of their thirty-day enlistment period, they went back to their homes. To attract recruits, Reynolds shortened the time of service to twenty days. There was some response and, by the middle of June, General Atkinson's command was made up of five hundred regular army troops and more than three thousand militiamen.

Scouts brought news of the new army to Black Hawk. At the invitation of some friendly Winnebago, he led his people north into what is now Wisconsin. Black Hawk made camp at Lake Koshkonong so the people could rest, but he knew they wouldn't be safe for long.

A runner brought word that Winnebago informers had gone to Atkinson and offered to guide the Americans to Black Hawk's camp. The general accepted the offer, but before he could catch up, the Sauk had headed for the Trembling Lands. This was an area of marshes and bogs stretching north and east of Lake Koshkonong. It was full of water plants and dog-willow trees. In places there were patches of ground that looked solid but would sink beneath a man's weight until his head was under water. Black Hawk knew that his people hadn't the strength to travel far, and he thought the Americans were not likely to track him into the dangerous swamps of the Trembling Lands.

Atkinson and his army followed the Winnebago, but when they reached Lake Koshkonong, the Sauk were gone. Atkinson must have wondered if he would ever get the promotion he hoped for. He was being out-maneuvered and out-generaled by a sixty-five-year-old Indian. Atkinson made camp four miles from the Trembling Lands and turned the search for Black Hawk over to an officer of the militia, Colonel Henry Dodge.

A scout rode into Black Hawk's camp to tell him that Dodge and an army of two thousand men were massed outside the Trembling Lands. Black Hawk was more interested in finding a home and food for his people than in fighting Americans. The women, children, and old people who had followed him were close to starving. They were reduced to eating the bark from trees. Many of his people were getting sick from the dampness. The time had come to leave the doubtful safety of the swamps.

The Sauk began to move west toward the Mississippi. Black Hawk had hoped to pick up the warriors and supplies that had been promised by the Winnebago and the Potawatomi just a month earlier. Most went back on their word. Black Hawk pleaded with chiefs he had known for years, but the answer was always the same—this was Black Hawk's war! It didn't belong to them, and they wanted no part of it. They had learned to be afraid of the Americans.

Black Hawk was alone. It wouldn't do any good to ask for help from the Sauk and Fox on the Iowa River. Keokuk was in charge there, and he was a friend of the Americans.

On July 21 Black Hawk brought his people to a shallow place on the Wisconsin River about forty miles from Fort Winnebago. There, it would be possible for the women, children, and old people to cross to safety. He knew that Dodge and his big army were close on his heels.

While the crossing was made, Neapope offered to take a small band of mounted warriors and act as a moving shield between the Sauk and the Americans. The country along the Wisconsin River was ideal for his purpose. It was a landscape clawed into ridges and deep ravines. Warriors could appear and disappear suddenly. Neapope and his men were able to lead the Americans first one way and then another, delaying them until Black Hawk was ready to fight.

In the late afternoon, when most of the people had crossed the river, a runner brought word that the Americans were massing on a ridge about a mile away. Black Hawk collected a band of warriors and went to help Neapope and the men who had done such a good job of delaying the enemy. He rode to the top of a hill where he could keep track of the action. The high, shrill voice of Black Hawk was heard directing and encouraging his warriors until the sun went down.

At nightfall the American militiamen looked at the high grass and the trees along the river and the ridges and dark ravines that lay inland. They remembered the stories that had been told about Stillman's Run. They refused to fight again until daylight.

Black Hawk was surprised when his enemy stopped the battle, but he was glad for the delay. It gave him the time he needed to get his warriors over to the other side of the Wisconsin River.

Only a few of his band had been hurt or killed. The wounded were rescued and the bodies of the slain were gathered up to be buried on the other side of the river. In the morning, when the Americans came out to start the fighting, all the Sauk, alive and dead, had disappeared.

General Atkinson was as angry with Colonel Dodge as he was with Black Hawk. The old Indian warrior had escaped again. Atkinson ordered an all-out pursuit of the Sauk. This time he took the command himself.

Black Hawk and his people headed northwest toward the

place where the Bad Axe River flows into the Mississippi. If they could get that far without being caught, they could cross into Iowa where the Americans said they wanted them to be. Surely, there the yellow earth people would be allowed to live in peace.

Black Hawk moved as fast as he could, but he had to go at a pace that would allow the children and old people to keep up. They must not be left to the mercy of the whites. His wife, Singing Bird, hurried up and down the line of march, helping the old people to walk, carrying the children, urging everybody to keep moving. Black Hawk's two sons were at the side of their father.

On August 1, 1832, the Sauk reached the place where the waters of the Bad Axe River flowed into the Mississippi. There, the father of waters was broken by islands and sand bars. If they were very careful, the people could get safely across. All was going well when, suddenly, a warrior pointed downstream on the Mississippi.

Coming toward the Indians was an armed steamboat, the *Warrior*. The keen eyes of Black Hawk recognized the pennant of the commander, Captain Joseph Throckmorton. Black Hawk knew Throckmorton, and he hoped the captain would help to ferry his people across the river.

When the *Warrior* was within hailing distance, Black Hawk held his hand high and waved a white flag of truce. He shouted his name and said that he wanted peace. The women and children gathered on the river bank were a sign that he meant what he said.

On board the *Warrior* there was a Winnebago who translated Indian words for the white men. We do not know what meaning he gave to Black Hawk's words. The boat was

Many brave Sauk and Fox people died in the Battle of the Bad Axe.

armed with a six-pound cannon loaded with small shot, and every man on board had a gun. They all opened fire on the Sauk gathered on the shore. Black Hawk's flag of truce was shot from his hand.

All night long the *Warrior* moved back and forth, bombarding the Wisconsin side of the river. Helpless people who tried to cross the Mississippi were caught in the wake of the great paddlewheel as it churned the water. They were drowned.

On the morning of August 2, General Atkinson, with two thousand regular army troops and militiamen, appeared on a bluff above the river. Some say that Black Hawk had escaped during the night. Others declare that he waited and offered to give himself up if his people were allowed to go in peace and safety. In any case, even though the Sauk were offering no signs of fighting back, the general ordered his troops to charge.

Later Black Hawk described what happened. "Our braves, but few in number, finding that the enemy paid no regard to age or sex, and seeing that they were murdering helpless women and little children, determined to fight until they were killed! As many women as could, [started] swimming the Mississippi, with their children on their backs. A number of them were drowned, and some shot, before they could reach the opposite shore."

No one knows how many people died in that battle on the Bad Axe River. By the end of the day, not one Sauk warrior was left alive on the field. But there was no sign of Black Hawk.

The Black Hawk War was over. The Sauk had suffered a defeat from which they could never recover. Black Hawk and his five hundred warriors had been beaten, but it had taken the combined efforts of the Illinois militia and the United States army and navy to do it.

Brevet General Henry Atkinson had won a war, but he didn't feel like a victor. The prize had escaped. When he lost Black Hawk, Atkinson lost the promotion for which he had hoped. He was still a general by courtesy only.

CHAPTER VII

Farewell
to My Nation

Black Hawk had a price on his head. The Americans knew that he and his friends had escaped to the north and were hiding among friendly Winnebago in Wisconsin. The Americans promised the Winnebago that they would be given twenty fine horses and two hundred dollars in cash if they would hand over Black Hawk. If they refused, part of their land would be taken away from them.

Black Hawk didn't want to be the cause of suffering to the people who were trying to be his friends. He said he would go to Prairie du Chien where Colonel Zachary Taylor was waiting to accept his surrender. The great Sauk leader didn't know what would happen to him when he gave himself up to the Americans. He was an enemy and he had been defeated. Perhaps they would kill him.

The Winnebago women made Black Hawk a fine hunting dress of soft white deerskin. Two warriors went with him to Prairie du Chien, where Taylor received the party with all courtesies due honored visitors.

The colonel admired Black Hawk as a warrior and a leader. Like most career military men, Taylor believed that the Black Hawk War had been unjust and that it had been forced on the Sauk by politicians. When Black Hawk looked

Black Hawk did not want his people to suffer on his account. At Prairie du Chien he surrendered to the American commander.

into the eyes of Zachary Taylor, he looked into the eyes of a friend.

The Galenian, a newspaper published in Illinois, sent a writer to cover the meeting between the Sauk leader and the American army officer. The story reported that Black Hawk stood proudly before Colonel Taylor and said,

"Black Hawk is an Indian! He has done nothing to make an Indian hang his head in shame."

He went on to say that Indians did not lie. Indians did not steal. White people could not make the same claims about themselves. If an Indian behaved the way the whites did, he would not be allowed to live in the tribe. Black Hawk had tried to save the Sauk. He had failed but he had done his duty. He was ready to give an accounting to the Great Spirit of how he had lived his life.

Fixing his gaze on a faraway place that no one else could see, the great Sauk warrior said in a firm voice,

"Farewell to my nation. Farewell to Black Hawk!"

The colonel made his prisoner comfortable and treated him like a guest. In a matter of weeks, the two sons of Black Hawk, Whirling Thunder and Roaring Thunder, along with Neapope and the Prophet, as well as what was left of the Sauk warriors, came to Prairie du Chien to give themselves up.

Before decisions could be made about what was to be done with them, cholera broke out in the town. Taylor thought that Black Hawk and the others would be safer if they were moved away from Prairie du Chien. He chose to send them to Jefferson Barracks outside Saint Louis. The Sauk were put in the charge of a young lieutenant, Jefferson Davis, for the journey.

The commandant of Jefferson Barracks was none other than Brevet General Henry Atkinson. Years before, the general had been in charge of building the barracks. Now, thanks to his failure in the Black Hawk affair, he was back where he had started.

When Lieutenant Davis delivered Black Hawk and the others to Jefferson Barracks, the general was face to face with the old man who had outwitted and outrun him. His first order was to put the Sauk leader in chains with a heavy iron ball attached to his ankle. The other Indians were treated the same way. If Atkinson could have done it, he probably would have locked up Black Hawk and the others in the barracks and forgotten about them. However, the people of Saint Louis demanded a chance to see the warrior who had become so famous. Atkinson found himself acting more like a host to a great man than a jailer. To control the crowds, he had to set up visiting hours.

The crowds were not happy with what they saw. They complained that Black Hawk did not jump about and rattle his chains as they had expected. Instead, he was a tired old man who sat quietly and gazed off into space, looking at something they could not see.

Black Hawk felt ashamed when people came to gawk and stare at him. If the general had been a prisoner of the Sauk, Indian custom would have protected him from that kind of dishonor.

It didn't take long for Atkinson to become tired of his prisoners and the attention they were getting from the townspeople. When word came that President Andrew Jackson wanted to meet Black Hawk, the general was relieved to see him go.

All the Sauk were set free except Black Hawk's sons and his friends, Neapope and the Prophet. Along with Black Hawk, they set out from Saint Louis for Fort Monroe at the mouth of the Chesapeake River in Maryland.

The party went by steamboat, stagecoach, and that new marvel, the railroad, on their way east. Black Hawk was interested in these strange means of travel, but he would have been more comfortable riding on the back of a horse.

When he arrived in Washington, the president made him wait three days before calling him to the White House. On April 25, 1833, the two old men faced each other.

Black Hawk and Jackson had been born the same year. Their faces, hearts, and bodies bore the scars of the battles they had fought, the disappointments they had faced, and the mistakes they had made. They were alike in one more way—hatred. Andrew Jackson hated Indians, and Black Hawk hated Americans.

Black Hawk had brought along a Sauk war bonnet of eagle feathers as a gift for the president. He had prepared a speech in which he planned to tell Jackson about the wrongs the Sauk had suffered and ask for understanding and respect.

The speech was never given. Jackson waved aside all the ceremonies of welcome. He glared at Black Hawk and demanded to know why the Sauk had made war against the United States. Black Hawk didn't know what to say. He thought the president already knew the answer to that question.

The Sauk found out that the journey to Washington had not been a courtesy between friends. They were only changing prisons—Jefferson Barracks for Fort Monroe. But there was a difference. At Fort Monroe, Black Hawk, his sons, and his friends were treated as guests. There were no chains and no balls of iron attached to their ankles. They were free to go where they pleased inside the walls of the fort.

Army officers, statesmen, and politicians came to visit the famous Black Hawk. Even Henry Clay, the famous speaker and statesman, came from Washington to spend some time with him. Artists and writers pleaded to be allowed to paint, draw, or talk to the prisoners. Wives of the officers at the fort sent baskets of provisions. The Sauk received the offerings politely but ate them only if the women were watching. They didn't like American food.

After six weeks at Fort Monroe, the federal government decided to send Black Hawk and the others on a tour. The idea was to impress them with the power and might of the United States so that, in the future, they would make no more trouble.

The Sauk visited Philadelphia and saw the United States Mint where the coins were made that had taken the place of the ancient wampum. They watched ships being built for the United States Navy. They craned their necks to watch a balloon filled with hot air lift off the ground, and they wondered at the people who had the courage to ride in the basket it carried.

The party visited New York City, Boston, Albany, Detroit, and places in between. Everywhere there were large and noisy crowds. Some were friendly. Some were so threatening that guards had to be placed around the Indians. At each stop on the tour, they were greeted by local public officials, honored at banquets, and forced to listen to long-winded speeches made up of words they couldn't understand.

They watched and wondered at the amounts of whiskey the Americans drank. The Sauk refused to touch it.

Black Hawk was tired, bored, and hungry. The food the Americans placed before him at the banquets didn't agree with him. He longed to go home.

When the tour reached Baltimore, President Jackson was in town. He sent for Black Hawk, and the two men met for the second time. The president told the Sauk warrior that he had decided to send him back to his people. The Sauk had been asked if they wanted Black Hawk to return, and the answer had been yes.

Jackson told the aging leader that he and his sons and friends were free to go back to their people. However, if Black Hawk didn't behave himself in the future, the Sauk would be the ones to suffer.

On August 2, 1833, just one year after the Battle of Bad Axe, Black Hawk came to the place on the Iowa River where his people were trying to make homes for themselves.

CHAPTER VIII

Black Hawk Remembered

The Sauk and Fox were no longer the proud tribes they had been when they lived in the valley of the Rock River. They had been forced to move to the west of the Mississippi where the earth had never been softened. It would be years before the land would yield harvests big enough to feed the people. To stay alive, they had become beggars at the doors of the trading posts.

Instead of counting coup, a man gained honor among his friends if he could drink more whiskey than anyone else before he lost his senses. Pride was gone. Honor was a memory.

Politicians demanded that the Indians pay damages for the Black Hawk War. The only thing of value left to the Sauk and Fox was land. The government forced chiefs to put their signs on a treaty that sold six million acres to the Americans. The land was a fifty-mile wide strip that stretched from what is now the northern border of Missouri to the southern edge of Minnesota. A small tract was set aside to be a reservation where the Sauk and Fox could build their houses and plant their fields.

Payment for the land did not come to the people. Instead, it was applied toward their bills at the trading posts. The deal became known as the Black Hawk Purchase although the Sauk leader had nothing to do with it.

Black Hawk came back to his nation and met his people at Fort Armstrong. When he saw what had happened while he was away, he couldn't bear the sight. He decided to leave the fort and, with a group of faithful Sauk who had been waiting for him, to settle near the present site of Eldon, Iowa.

When Black Hawk tried to leave Fort Armstrong, he found out that the Americans had tricked him. He was not free to go and come as he pleased. The Americans had paroled him in the custody of his enemy, Keokuk. Black Hawk would rather have died in prison. He would never fight again.

Keokuk made no trouble when Black Hawk said he wanted to leave the fort. Indeed, he was glad to see the old man go. Too many people admired Black Hawk and disliked Keokuk.

Black Hawk no longer took part in tribal affairs. Even when the people tried to replace Keokuk with Black Hawk's eldest son, he held his tongue. Keokuk found out about the plan, and, with the help of the Americans, he crushed it.

Black Hawk's last public appearance was at a July Fourth celebration in Fort Madison. As an honored guest, he sat with the important people who had come to make speeches. The commandant of Fort Madison offered a toast to Black Hawk. In reply, the old Sauk warrior asked the Americans to treasure the valley of the Rock River. It had been a good home for the yellow earth people.

Black Hawk became ill with a fever and died on October 3, 1838. He was seventy-one years old. Although he was not a chief, the yellow earth people buried him with all the honors and rituals that went with the burial of a sacred chief. A wooden post carved with the symbols of the Thunder clan was at the foot of the grave.

Not even death, however, could protect Black Hawk from the Americans. His body was stolen from the grave by James Turner, a local doctor. Turner fled across the Mississippi River to Illinois where he thought he would be out of the reach of Iowa law. He planned to make a fortune showing the bones of Black Hawk in eastern museums and traveling shows.

As soon as the theft was discovered, the governor of the Iowa Territory demanded that Illinois take the proper action to return the remains of the Sauk leader. Black Hawk was such a famous figure to Iowans that his return became a popular cause. When a newspaper editor suggested that Iowa be called the "Hawkeye State" in his honor, it wasn't long before the lawmakers made the name official. Iowa residents still speak of themselves as Hawkeyes.

The uproar in Iowa caused Illinois to return the remains of Black Hawk. However, his family refused to accept them. The soul of Black Hawk was with the Great Spirit. What was left of his body had been defiled by the Americans and could not be placed in sacred burial grounds.

The remains were turned over to the Iowa Historical Society in Burlington for safekeeping. A few years later, the society's building burned to the ground. At last Black Hawk was free of the Americans.

The Indians were still at the mercy of the whites. Andrew Jackson and the American presidents who followed him wanted the Indians out of the way. The land on which they lived was valuable, and homesteaders were demanding that it be opened for settlement.

By order of the federal government, the Indians were moved out of their homes in the eastern mountains, valleys, and forests. With U.S. troops as an escort, they were transported to the dusty lands of the Southwest. Whole nations were driven out with only the possessions they could carry. Everything else was left for the settlers who took over their lands.

Many people died on the way west. The Potowatomi called the sad trip the Trail of Death. The Cherokee, Choctaw, and Creek called it the Trail of Tears.

In 1846 it was the turn of the yellow earth and the red earth peoples to leave their homes in Iowa and join the Trail of Tears. The Sauk and Fox who lived through the journey were put on a reservation near the headwaters of the Osage River in the Territory of Kansas. Not even Keokuk was spared. He traveled with the rest and died on the Kansas reservation in 1847.

Some of the Americans whose actions and decisions touched the life of Black Hawk are mentioned in history books.

William Henry Harrison, who sowed the first seeds of the Black Hawk War with the Treaty of 1804, went on to become the ninth president of the United States.

Zachary Taylor, whom Black Hawk defeated at Saukenuk and who, later, received the surrender of the great Sauk leader, became the twelfth United States president.

Jefferson Davis, who escorted Black Hawk from Fort Armstrong to Jefferson Barracks, became president of the Southern Confederacy in the War Between The States. It

On the top of a bluff overlooking the Rock River stands
a monument to the Sauk warrior and patriot, Black Hawk.

is said that, after the defeat of the South, Davis was placed in the same cell at Jefferson Barracks in which Black Hawk had been confined.

One lanky young man joined Governor Reynold's Illinois militia because, as he wrote to a friend, he needed the money. His name was Abraham Lincoln. He became the sixteenth president of the United States. During the Civil War he was the leader who held the Union together.

All these men have monuments to their memories. Black Hawk, the Sauk Indian whose life they touched, has them, too. Near the city of Rock Island, Illinois, an area of rolling lands has been set aside as a state park. It is dedicated to the memory of Black Hawk.

In 1911 the famous American sculptor, Lorado Taft, designed a tribute to the last great Sauk warrior. A statue, carved in stone, stands fifty feet high and overlooks the valley of the Rock River where the people of the yellow earth once lived happily. Black Hawk is remembered!

THE AUTHOR

A free-lance writer and commercial artist, Maggi Cunningham has written many short stories, including stories about native Americans, for children's magazines. This is her third book. The first two, *The Cherokee Tale-Teller* and *Little Turtle, The Story of an American Indian,* are also published by Dillon Press.

She spent her childhood in Washington State, North Dakota, and Minnesota— states with a rich Indian tradition—to which she credits her interest in native American culture. Ms. Cunningham was educated at Saint Margaret's Academy in Minneapolis, Saint Mary of the Springs in Columbus, Ohio, and Ohio State University. She is now living in Columbus.

Photographs reproduced through the courtesy of the Chicago Historical Society, the Field Museum of Natural History and George Catlin, the Iowa Department of History and Archives, the State Historical Society of Iowa, the Ohio Historical Society, the National Anthropological Archives and the National Collection of Fine Arts of the Smithsonian Institution, and the State Historical Society of Wisconsin.

OTHER BIOGRAPHIES
IN THIS SERIES ARE

William Beltz
Robert Bennett
Joseph Brant
Charles Eastman
Crazy Horse
Geronimo
Oscar Howe
Ishi
Pauline Johnson
Chief Joseph
Little Turtle
Maria Martinez
George Morrison
Daisy Hooee Nampeyo
Michael Naranjo
Osceola
Powhatan
Red Cloud
Will Rogers
John Ross
Sacagawea
Sealth
Sequoyah
Sitting Bull
Maria Tallchief
Tecumseh
Jim Thorpe
Tomo-chi-chi
Pablita Velarde
William Warren
Alford Waters
Annie Wauneka
Wovoka